KOALAS

Published by Creative Education, Inc., 123 South Broad Street, Mankato, Minnesota
56001

Printed by permission of Wildlife Education, Ltd.

ISBN 0-88682-227-0

KOALAS

Created and Written by
John Bonnett Wexo

Zoological Consultant
Charles R. Schroeder, D.V.M.
Director Emeritus
San Diego Zoo &
San Diego Wild Animal Park

Scientific Consultants
Phillip T. Robinson, M.S., D.V.M.
Director of Veterinary Services
San Diego Zoo

Jane Jacobson
Koala Keeper
San Diego Zoo

Creative Education

Art Credits

Pages Eight and Nine: Karel Havlicek; **Page Eight: Lower Left,** Walter Stuart; **Page Nine: Lower Right,** Dave Christensen; **Pages Ten and Eleven:** Walter Stuart; **Page Eleven: Upper Left and Lower Right,** Karel Havlicek; **Pages Twelve and Thirteen:** Karel Havlicek; **Page Thirteen: Upper Right,** Walter Stuart; **Pages Sixteen and Seventeen:** Karel Havlicek; **Pages Eighteen and Nineteen:** Karel Havlicek; **Page Nineteen: Center and Bottom,** Walter Stuart; **Pages Twenty and Twenty-One:** Karel Havlicek; **Page Twenty: Upper Right,** Karl Edwards; **Page Twenty-One: Bottom,** Walter Stuart; **Pages Twenty-Two and Twenty-Three:** Karel Havlicek; **Inset Boxes,** Walter Stuart; **Page Twenty-Two: Upper Right and Bottom,** Walter Stuart; **Page Twenty-Three: Lower Right,** Walter Stuart.

Photographic Credits

Cover: Jean-Paul Ferrero *(Ardea London);* **Pages Six and Seven:** Eckart Pott *(Bruce Coleman, Ltd.);* **Page Nine:** Jen and Des Bartlett *(Bruce Coleman, Ltd.);* **Page Ten:** R.M. Maratea *(Shostal Associates);* **Page Eleven:** Peter Morris *(Ardea London);* **Page Twelve: Upper Left,** Brian Brake *(Photo Researchers);* **Lower Left,** Courtesy of Qantas Airways, Ltd.; **Page Thirteen:** Courtesy of Qantas Airways, Ltd.; **Pages Fourteen and Fifteen:** John G. Herron *(Aperture);* **Page Eighteen: Top Right,** G. Ziesler *(Bruce Coleman, Ltd.);* **Lower Left,** Courtesy of Australian Information Service/Australian Consulate; **Page Twenty:** Jean-Paul Ferrero *(Ardea London);* **Lower Right,** Stephen J. Krasemann *(DRK Photos);* **Page Twenty-Three: Upper Right,** *(series of three)* W.R. Taylor *(Ardea London);* **Lower Left,** Jean-Paul Ferrero *(Ardea London).*

Our Thanks To: Dr. Marilyn Anderson *(San Diego Zoo);* Doug Atkins *(Quantas Airways);* Chris Banks *(Royal Melbourne Zoo);* Dr. E.C. Boterenbrood *(Hubrecht Laboratorium, The Netherlands);* Mary Byrd *(San Diego Zoo);* Ernie Chew; Dr. Phil Ensley *(San Diego Zoo);* R.A. Fairfax *(South Perth Zoological Gardens);* Mary Fotheringham *(MacMillan Company of Australia);* Dr. Paul Hopwood *(University of Sydney);* Dr. Masaharu Horiguchi *(Tohoku University, Japan);* Dr. Leon Hughes *(University of Queensland);* Wade Hughes; Mrs. N.W. Keith *(Australian Institute of Anatomy);* A.G. Lyne *(Division of Wildlife Research, Australia);* John H. Miles, Jr. *(Smithsonian Institution);* Dr. Ralph Molnar *(Queensland Museum);* Dr. Alan Nadham and Diane Thomas *(University of New South Wales);* Dr. Donald Patten *(Los Angeles County Natural History Museum);* Brian Peck and Ursula Garvey *(Australian Information Service);* Michaele Robinson *(San Diego Zoo);* Stacey Rosenfield; Dr. Lynne Selwood *(La Trobe University, Australia);* Dr. Ronald Strahan *(The Australian Museum);* Robert Ward and Danny Simpson *(San Diego Zoo Horticultural Department);* A.G. Wells *(Wildlife Photos, Australia);* Steve Willie and Pat Ontiveros *(Cunningham and Walsh);* Lynnette Wexo.

Creative Education would like to thank Wildlife Education, Ltd., for granting them the rights to print and distribute this hardbound edition.

Contents

Koalas are certainly near the top of everybody's list of "the world's cutest animals." And it's easy to see why people love them. They are covered with thick and fuzzy fur, and look like they were *made* to be cuddled. Most of the time, they have a sleepy and friendly look about them. In fact, koalas look so much like living teddy bears that many people still call them koala *bears*.

But koalas are not bears. They are not even closely related to bears. Instead, they belong to an unusual group of mammals called marsupials (MAR-SOUP-EE-ULS). Like other marsupials (and *unlike* bears), koalas have pouches that they use for carrying their babies.

To see koalas in their natural home, you have to go to Australia. And you will only be able to find them in areas where certain types of trees are growing. Koalas only eat the leaves of eucalyptus (YOU-KAH-LIP-TUS) trees, and they only live where eucalyptus trees grow.

Koalas are *very* fussy about the kinds of eucalyptus leaves they will eat. There are over 600 kinds of eucalyptus trees growing in all parts of Australia, but koalas only eat the leaves of 35 kinds that grow in eastern Australia. Some koalas will eat only *two or three* kinds of leaves. If they can't find the leaves they like, they will simply not eat.

This is why koalas have disappeared from many areas in the past. Eucalyptus trees have been cut down to make room for farms, and the koalas could not find food.

Over the years, zoos around the world have tried to keep koalas, but most of them have failed because they could not give the koalas enough eucalyptus leaves. Today, koalas can be seen at only a few zoos outside Australia. This is because these zoos have been able to grow eucalyptus trees or can get leaves to feed them.

Koalas are nocturnal animals (KNOCK-TURN-UL). This means that they usually sleep during the day and are awake during the night. Most people only get to see koalas when they are sleeping in the daytime, and this is why many people think that koalas are very lazy animals.

A fully grown koala may be 3 feet long, but most adults are about 2 feet long (61 centimeters). Koalas weigh between 10 and 30 pounds (4.5 kilograms and 13.6 kilograms). Nobody is really sure how long they live in nature, but they may live for 20 years or more.

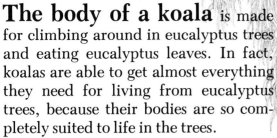

The body of a koala is made for climbing around in eucalyptus trees and eating eucalyptus leaves. In fact, koalas are able to get almost everything they need for living from eucalyptus trees, because their bodies are so completely suited to life in the trees.

For example, eucalyptus leaves are poisonous to most mammals, but koalas can eat them. They have special stomachs that can break down the poisonous oils in the leaves. So the average koala can eat about 2½ pounds of "poison" leaves every day, with no problems.

Koalas can also get most of the water they need by eating the leaves. At certain times of the year, eucalyptus leaves may be almost ⅔ water. So a koala can munch on leaves and go for months without actually drinking any water. (Many people say that the name "koala" is a native Australian word meaning "does not drink.")

High up in the trees, it can get very windy. To keep them warm, koalas have very thick fur on their backs. The ability of fur to keep an animal warm is called its "insulating ability." Koala fur has the best insulating ability of any marsupial fur that scientists have tested so far.

Koalas may look soft and cuddly, but under the fur they have a lot of muscle. They need it for hanging on to trees and climbing around all night. Like trapeze artists in a circus, much of their muscle is concentrated in their arms and shoulders.

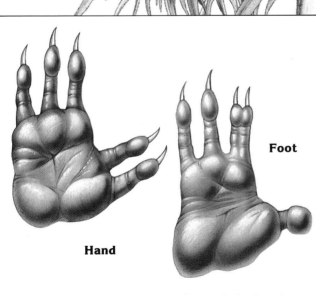

Foot

Hand

Koalas have special hands and feet to help them hang on tight when they climb trees. To get a really good grip on branches, they have *two* thumbs on each hand. (How tight do you think you could grab a branch if *you* had two thumbs on each hand?) Koalas also use their feet to hold on—and both the hands and the feet have sharp claws on them. With all of this climbing equipment, koalas seldom fall out of trees.

Marsupial Bones

When you look at the skeleton of a koala, it's easy to see that a koala is a marsupial. It has two bones attached to its hip bones that only marsupials have. These bones help to hold up the pouch in female marsupials, and they are called "marsupial bones." Males don't have pouches, but they also have marsupial bones.

The big nose of a koala helps the animal decide what to eat. A koala sniffs every leaf before eating it, to be sure it is fit to eat. If it doesn't smell exactly right, the koala will pass it by.

The body of a kangaroo is made for hopping around on the ground. For this reason, most of the muscle is located at the back end—in the huge legs and tail. All of this muscle is used for hopping, but it can also be used for fighting. When kangaroos fight, they often sit back on their tails, so that they can use both of their big feet to kick and scratch. As you can imagine, they pack a big punch—and the claws on the feet can be deadly.

Baby koalas and other baby marsupials start life in a different way from most of the other mammals on earth. In fact, the main difference between marsupials and other mammals is the way in which their babies are born. Koalas and other marsupials give birth to "unfinished" babies, and then carry them around in pouches for a time. (The word "marsupial" means "pouched animal.") Most other mammals are called placental mammals (PLUH-SENT-ul). They give birth to more "finished" babies and do not have pouches.

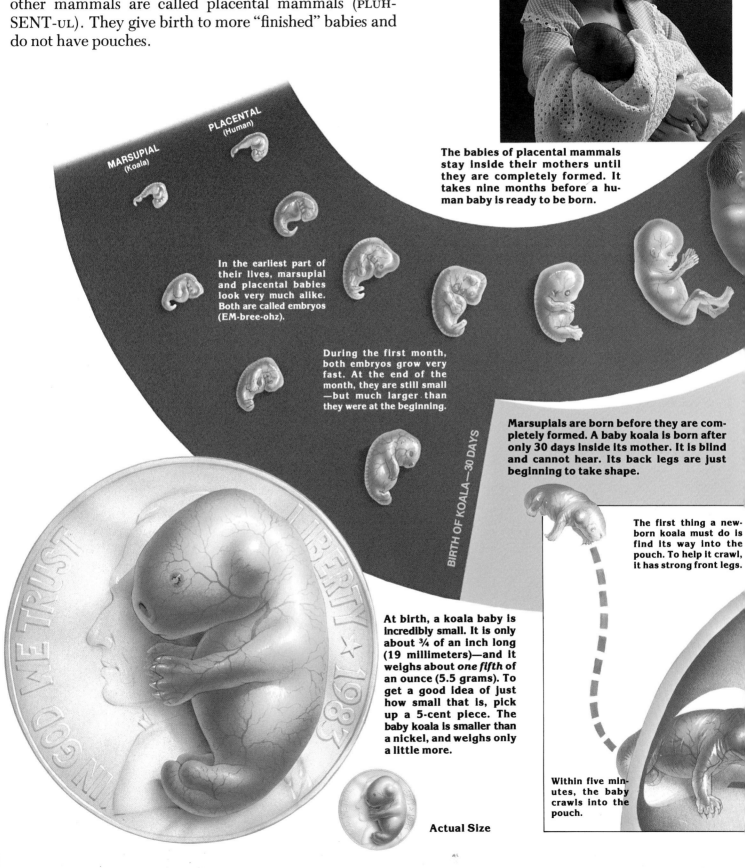

The babies of placental mammals stay inside their mothers until they are completely formed. It takes nine months before a human baby is ready to be born.

MARSUPIAL (Koala)

PLACENTAL (Human)

In the earliest part of their lives, marsupial and placental babies look very much alike. Both are called embryos (EM-bree-ohz).

During the first month, both embryos grow very fast. At the end of the month, they are still small —but much larger than they were at the beginning.

BIRTH OF KOALA—30 DAYS

Marsupials are born before they are completely formed. A baby koala is born after only 30 days inside its mother. It is blind and cannot hear. Its back legs are just beginning to take shape.

The first thing a newborn koala must do is find its way into the pouch. To help it crawl, it has strong front legs.

At birth, a koala baby is incredibly small. It is only about ¾ of an inch long (19 millimeters)—and it weighs about *one fifth* of an ounce (5.5 grams). To get a good idea of just how small that is, pick up a 5-cent piece. The baby koala is smaller than a nickel, and weighs only a little more.

Actual Size

Within five minutes, the baby crawls into the pouch.

By the time a young koala comes out of the pouch for the first time, it is about 8 inches long (20 centimeters) and covered with fur. Unlike most other marsupials, koalas have pouches that open toward the back.

For two months after it first comes out of the pouch, a baby koala still uses it as a place to sleep—and a place to hide in. When anything frightens it, the baby pops into the pouch. From the safety of the pouch, it peers out to see what's going on.

People used to think that the marsupial way of having babies was not as good as the placental way. But now most scientists feel that both ways may be equally good. One advantage of the pouch method is that the mother never has to leave her baby when she goes to find food. The baby rides with her in the safety of the pouch.

BIRTH OF HUMAN—9 MONTHS

The six months that a koala spends in the pouch are like the last six months that a human baby spends inside its mother. The baby grows larger and stronger, and gets ready to come out into the world.

When baby koalas get too big to fit into the pouch, their mothers start carrying them on their backs. By this time, the hands and feet of the baby are already very strong. They are able to hold on to their mothers with a very tight grip.

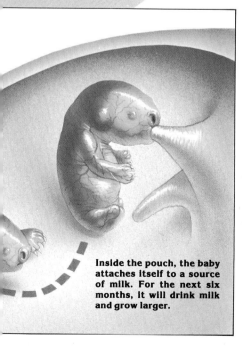

Inside the pouch, the baby attaches itself to a source of milk. For the next six months, it will drink milk and grow larger.

Baby koalas start eating eucalyptus leaves soon after they come out of the pouch for the first time. They also continue taking milk from their mothers until they are about a year old. When they stop taking milk and eat only eucalyptus leaves, they are grown up enough to go out on their own.

When a koala isn't eating, it is usually sleeping. Unlike most other marsupials that live in trees, koalas do not have nests. They simply wrap themselves around a branch or snuggle into the fork of a tree and doze off.

Koalas may *look* lazy, but when it comes to getting food, they will sometimes put out an astonishing amount of energy. They may climb more than 150 feet (45 meters) to the swaying top of a eucalyptus tree—or they may even leap through the air to a new tree.

As some zoo keepers could tell you, koalas aren't always as cuddly and friendly as they look. They can have very quick tempers. When they are left alone, they seem content to mind their own business. But if they feel that some-body is bothering them too much, they may scratch with their long claws—or they may grind a human finger or two between their teeth. When a koala is in a bad mood, it will sometimes make a very loud and fast ticking sound—like a time-bomb ticking.

Koalas don't often come down from the trees. But sometimes, if there is no other way to reach a new food tree, or if they want to drink water from a stream, they do climb down. They aren't comfortable on the ground, and they walk with an awkward swaying motion. But if they are chased, they can run almost as fast as a rabbit. Oddly enough, these tree-living animals are also good swimmers.

In Australia, people try to take good care of their koalas. In places where koalas must cross a road to get to feeding grounds, there are even signs warning drivers to be careful.

Koalas that live in different parts of eastern Australia look different from each other, and they eat different kinds of eucalyptus leaves. If you take a koala from one place to another, you must also take a supply of eucalyptus leaves with you—because the koala will probably not eat the kinds of leaves growing in the new place. In general, koalas that live in the south are bigger than those that live in the north.

QUEENSLAND KOALA
Phascolarctos cinereus adustus

In general, koalas that live in warmer climates have less fur than koalas that live in cooler places. The Queensland Koala lives in one of the warmest parts of Australia, and its fur is the thinnest of all koalas. (In Australia, the farther north you go, the warmer it gets, because the country is located south of the equator.)

VICTORIA KOALA
Phascolarctos cinereus victor

NEW SOUTH WALES KOALA
Phascolarctos cinereus cinereus

The Victoria Koala lives in one of the coldest parts of Australia. It has very thick and shaggy fur. The dark color of the fur absorbs more heat from the sun than a lighter coat would, so it helps to keep the animal warm. Victoria koalas are the largest of all koalas.

The first type of koala to be discovered was the New South Wales Koala—and it is still the koala most people think of as the "typical" koala. It has a darker grey coat than the Queensland Koala, and the fur is thicker.

13

There are many kinds of marsupials

living in Australia and on nearby islands—more than 170 different species. And one of the first things that has to be said about them is that they are a remarkably *varied* group. There are marsupials of many different shapes, and sizes, and colors.

The reason for this is not hard to see. In general, the way an animal looks and behaves has to do with the kind of place it lives in and the way it gets its food. Australia has many different kinds of places for animals to live, from deserts to tropical forests—and so there are many different kinds of animals.

All marsupials in Australia are descended from animals that came to Australia more than 50 million years ago. After that time, Australia was cut off from the other continents of the world, and no other mammals were able to enter for a long time. For this reason, Australian marsupials are not even distantly related to placental mammals found in the rest of the world.

Oddly enough, some marsupials *look* and *behave* very much like some placental mammals that live in other parts of the world. If they aren't related, how can they be so similar? The answer can be found in the way the animals live—they are so much alike because *they live similar lives*. Sometimes, marsupial and placental mammals that live in similar places may be almost exactly alike. Other times, they may be alike in only a few ways—as you will see when you look at the pairs of animals shown on these pages.

GIANT ANT-EATER
Myrmecophaga tridactyla

BANDED ANT-EATER (OR NUMBAT)
Myrmecobius fasciatus
(Marsupial)

Common Wombats and Groundhogs are diggers. They live underground in burrows that can be very large. Both animals like to eat grass and are usually found living in forests or at the edge of forests.

GROUNDHOG
Marmota monax

COMMON WOMBAT
Vombatus hirsutus
(Marsupial)

INDRI
Indri indri

KOALA
Phascolarctos cinereus
(Marsupial)

DESERT SHREW
Notiosorex crawfordi

Both of these small desert animals eat insects. They live in holes, sleep during the heat of the day, and come out at night to find their food.

MARSUPIAL MOUSE
Antechinus macdonnellensis
(Marsupial)

TASMANIAN WOLF
Thylacinus cynocephalus
(Marsupial)

The Indri of Madagascar and the Koala look very much alike, and both animals spend most of their time up in trees. Both have long arms and legs, and feet that can grab branches tightly. Both have no tails, and both eat leaves. In other ways, they are very different. The Koala is awake at night, for example, while the Indri is awake during the day.

The "wolf" of Tasmania was the largest of the meat-eating marsupials. It looked very much like a North American wolf and ran on its toes like a wolf—a very unusual way of running for a marsupial. Like North American wolves, these animals often chased their prey for hours, waiting for the prey to get tired before attacking it. And they lived in lairs, like North American wolves. Nobody has seen a Tasmanian wolf for more than 30 years, and most people feel that they are extinct.

The Banded Ant-eater and the Giant Ant-eater are misnamed, because both of them prefer to eat termites. To help them do it, they both have long noses, sticky tongues, and strong claws on their front feet. The claws break into a termite nest, the nose hunts for termites in holes, and the tongue traps termites by the hundreds.

SPIDER MONKEY
Ateles paniscus

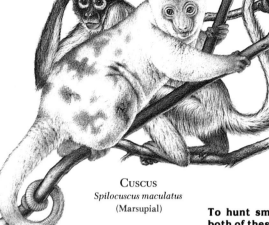

An extra "hand" is a good thing to have if you live up in the trees. The Cuscus (KUSS-kuss) and the Spider Monkey both have prehensile tails that they use like hands to hang on to branches. In most other ways, they are very different.

STAR-NOSED MOLE
Condylura cristata

MARSUPIAL MOLE
Notoryctes typhlops
(Marsupial)

CUSCUS
Spilocuscus maculatus
(Marsupial)

To hunt small animals in the forest, both of these animals have sharp teeth and a ferocious nature. The Tiger Cat does most of its hunting in the trees, while the Weasel hunts on the ground.

The two animals above look so much alike that it's really hard to believe that they aren't close relatives. Their lives are also very similar. They both dig tunnels with big claws on their front feet. Both have sensitive noses to help them "sniff out" good places to dig. Both eat tremendous amounts of food every day and spend most of their time rushing around after food.

TIGER CAT
Dasyurus maculatus
(Marsupial)

COMMON WEASEL
Mustela nivalus

RACCOON
Procyon lotor

BRUSH-TAILED POSSUM
Trichosurus vulpecula
(Marsupial)

When they can get it, Red Kangaroos eat grass like cows. And even though the kangaroo doesn't look much like a cow on the outside, it has certain parts inside that are very much like some parts of a cow. It has broad teeth, for example, for crushing tough plant fiber. And it has a cow-like stomach for digesting the fiber.

WOLF
Canis lupus

The Brush-tailed Possum and the Raccoon look very much alike, and have very similar lives. Both can live in a wide variety of different places and eat a wide variety of foods . . . and both are very good at keeping themselves hidden. For these reasons, both animals do very well living close to people. When other animals can no longer live in an area because people have changed it, these animals move in and make themselves comfortable.

DOMESTIC COW
Bos primigenius taurus

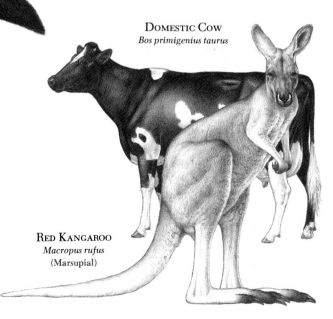

RED KANGAROO
Macropus rufus
(Marsupial)

Kangaroos are probably the most famous jumping animals in the world. Almost everybody has seen a picture of a big kangaroo jumping at great speed on the plains of Australia. The largest kangaroos are the biggest hopping animals on earth today — and they are also the largest of all marsupials. A big Red kangaroo can stand almost 7 feet tall (2 meters), and a Grey kangaroo can weigh 200 pounds (90 kilograms).

Like many other marsupials, kangaroos are plant-eaters, and they usually eat at night. They are sociable, and are often found in small groups called "mobs." A fully grown male is called a *boomer*. A female is a *doe*. And a young kangaroo of either sex is called a *joey*. Most kangaroos live to be about 7 years old — but some may live up to 20 years.

The front legs of kangaroos are usually much shorter than their back legs. But tree kangaroos are different. Their front legs are almost as long as their back legs, to help them climb around in trees. These wonderful animals can leap more than 30 feet (9 meters) from branch to branch. And they can jump 60 feet (18 meters) down to the ground without getting hurt. They land on all four feet, like a cat.

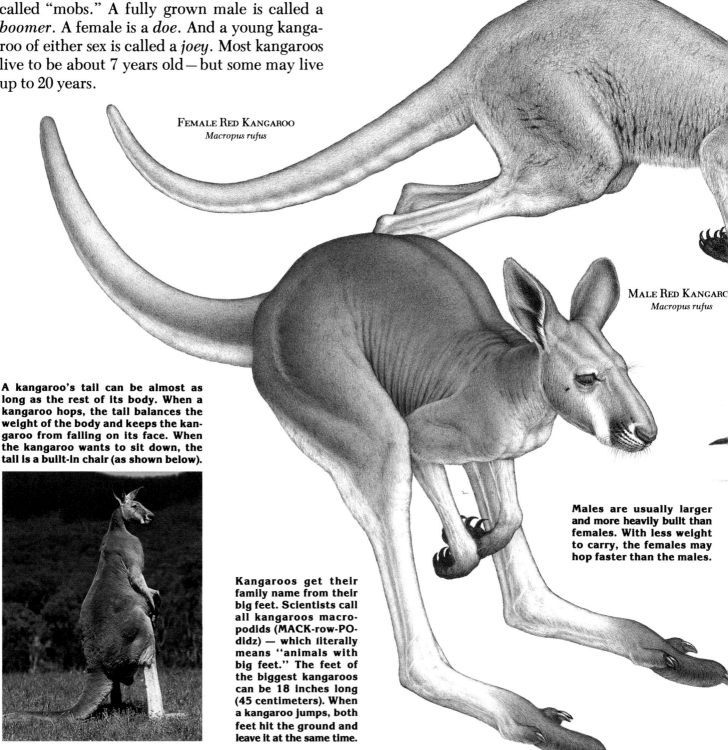

FEMALE RED KANGAROO
Macropus rufus

MALE RED KANGAROO
Macropus rufus

A kangaroo's tail can be almost as long as the rest of its body. When a kangaroo hops, the tail balances the weight of the body and keeps the kangaroo from falling on its face. When the kangaroo wants to sit down, the tail is a built-in chair (as shown below).

Kangaroos get their family name from their big feet. Scientists call all kangaroos macropodids (MACK-row-PO-didz) — which literally means "animals with big feet." The feet of the biggest kangaroos can be 18 inches long (45 centimeters). When a kangaroo jumps, both feet hit the ground and leave it at the same time.

Males are usually larger and more heavily built than females. With less weight to carry, the females may hop faster than the males.

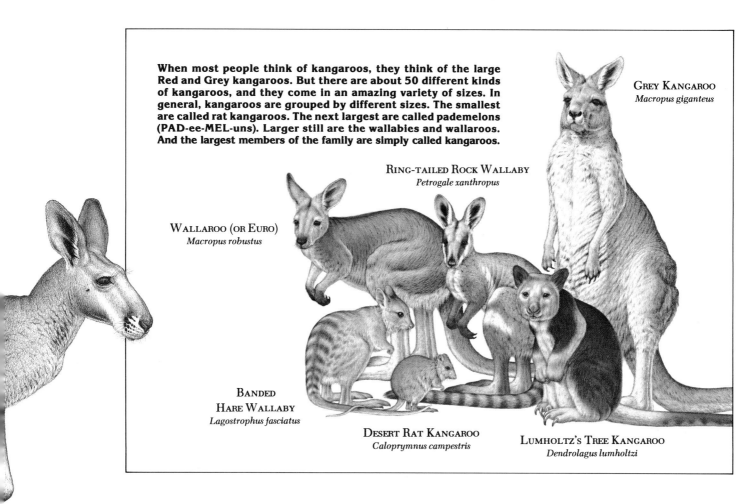

When most people think of kangaroos, they think of the large Red and Grey kangaroos. But there are about 50 different kinds of kangaroos, and they come in an amazing variety of sizes. In general, kangaroos are grouped by different sizes. The smallest are called rat kangaroos. The next largest are called pademelons (PAD-ee-MEL-uns). Larger still are the wallabies and wallaroos. And the largest members of the family are simply called kangaroos.

GREY KANGAROO
Macropus giganteus

RING-TAILED ROCK WALLABY
Petrogale xanthropus

WALLAROO (OR EURO)
Macropus robustus

BANDED
HARE WALLABY
Lagostrophus fasciatus

DESERT RAT KANGAROO
Caloprymnus campestris

LUMHOLTZ'S TREE KANGAROO
Dendrolagus lumholtzi

As strange as it may look, hopping is really a very good way of getting around. Large kangaroos can hop faster than horses can run. For short distances, they can move along at 40 miles per hour (64 kilometers per hour). To increase their speed, they simply take bigger and bigger hops.

No other animal on earth can jump as far as a big kangaroo can. Grey kangaroos have been known to jump 44 feet (13.5 meters) at a single bound. They can also leap over a fence that is 11 feet high (3.3 meters).

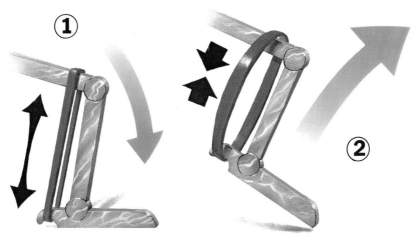

The kangaroo is the only animal known to science that actually uses *less* energy as it moves faster and faster. This is because kangaroos have a unique ability to recycle energy. When the foot of a kangaroo hits the ground, a large tendon in the leg is stretched like a rubber band ①. As the kangaroo leaves the ground again, the tendon "snaps back" and helps to lift the animal into the air ②.

As the kangaroo hops faster and faster, the "rubber band" snaps back faster and harder. More energy is stored and released in every hop. At speeds over 9 miles per hour (14 kilometers), almost two-thirds of the energy used is recycled through the leg tendons and other parts of the body. For this reason, a kangaroo can hop for a very long time before it gets tired.

The secret of success for kangaroos has been the wonderful ability of different kinds of kangaroos to live in different kinds of places. Wherever you go in Australia, you will probably find some kind of kangaroo living there. Members of the family thrive in deserts and rain forests, woods and grassy plains, scrubland and rocky areas. They are found where it is hot and where it is cold, where it is dry and where it is wet. They often eat food that other animals can't eat. In a word, kangaroos are very *flexible*—and this is why most scientists think that they are the most successful of all marsupials.

QUESTION: What would a kangaroo prefer to eat—a pile of grass or a box full of grass?

ANSWER: The kangaroo might prefer *the box* of grass—because some kangaroos love to eat cardboard boxes! There is a lot of cellulose (SELL-you-low-s) in cardboard, and kangaroos like to eat this tough plant fiber.

The front paws of kangaroos are sometimes used like hands. Kangaroos may pick up food with them or use them to comb dirt out of their fur. At times, a kangaroo will lick its paws and run them over its fur, just like a cat. There are also special claws on the big back feet that are used for cleaning the fur.

BETTONGS
Bettongia lesueur

Large kangaroos don't usually stay in one place for very long, and don't build homes for themselves. They spend most of their time wandering around looking for food and water. Small kangaroos don't move around so much, and often build nests. One small rat kangaroo, the Bettong, even digs out an underground home that looks like a rabbit hole.

When most people think about animals that need very little water to live, they think of the camel. But kangaroos that live in deserts can live on less water than camels. If necessary, the kangaroos can go for a week or more without drinking a drop.

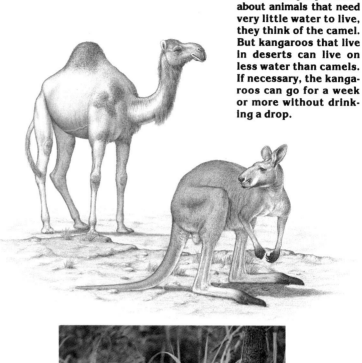

Some kangaroos live like mountain goats. These Rock wallabies have no fear of high places. They jump around on cliffs and never seem to fall. Even though they are only as big as large house cats, they can leap more than 13 feet (4 meters) from rock to rock.

PRETTY-FACE WALLABY
Wallabia elegans

The pouch of a female kangaroo is used in the same way as the pouch of the koala—except that the pouch opens toward the front instead of the back. For the first six months of its life, a baby kangaroo doesn't leave the pouch at all. For a few months after that, it jumps back into the pouch whenever it feels in danger or needs a rest. When it grows too large to get its whole body back into the pouch, it gets milk from its mother by sticking its head back into the pouch.

To protect themselves from predators, kangaroos that live in deserts or grasslands can run away. Kangaroos that live in trees or on rocky cliffs can climb up to a safe place. But kangaroos that live in dense forests and swamps usually protect themselves by standing still. They hide quietly among the trees and bushes, like deer. The Black-tailed wallaby shown above has a dark coat to help it hide in the forest shadows.

Kangaroos are powerful swimmers. They can easily swim across rivers and may even be seen swimming in the ocean. In water, a kangaroo kicks its legs differently than it does on land. Instead of moving both big legs at the same time, it moves one leg at a time.

Sometimes, large Red and Grey kangaroos will protect themselves from hunting dogs by leaping into a river or lake and swimming to deep water. If the dogs swim after them, the kangaroos grab the dogs and hold their heads under the water until they drown.

21

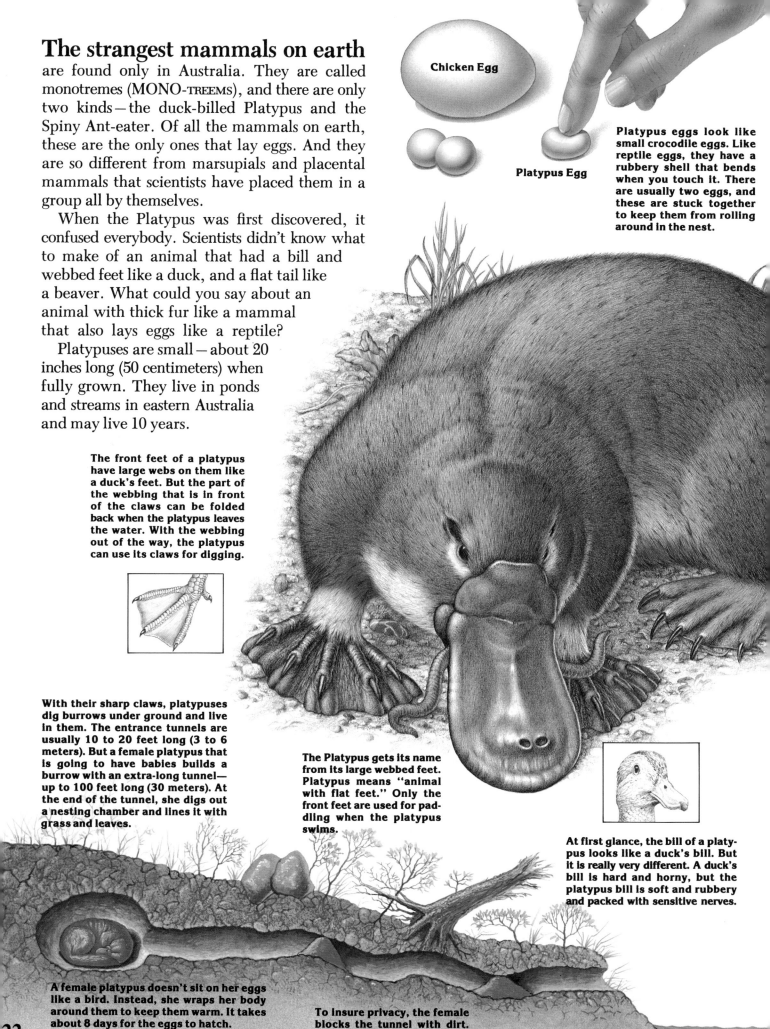

The strangest mammals on earth

are found only in Australia. They are called monotremes (MONO-TREEMS), and there are only two kinds—the duck-billed Platypus and the Spiny Ant-eater. Of all the mammals on earth, these are the only ones that lay eggs. And they are so different from marsupials and placental mammals that scientists have placed them in a group all by themselves.

When the Platypus was first discovered, it confused everybody. Scientists didn't know what to make of an animal that had a bill and webbed feet like a duck, and a flat tail like a beaver. What could you say about an animal with thick fur like a mammal that also lays eggs like a reptile?

Platypuses are small—about 20 inches long (50 centimeters) when fully grown. They live in ponds and streams in eastern Australia and may live 10 years.

Chicken Egg

Platypus Egg

Platypus eggs look like small crocodile eggs. Like reptile eggs, they have a rubbery shell that bends when you touch it. There are usually two eggs, and these are stuck together to keep them from rolling around in the nest.

The front feet of a platypus have large webs on them like a duck's feet. But the part of the webbing that is in front of the claws can be folded back when the platypus leaves the water. With the webbing out of the way, the platypus can use its claws for digging.

With their sharp claws, platypuses dig burrows under ground and live in them. The entrance tunnels are usually 10 to 20 feet long (3 to 6 meters). But a female platypus that is going to have babies builds a burrow with an extra-long tunnel—up to 100 feet long (30 meters). At the end of the tunnel, she digs out a nesting chamber and lines it with grass and leaves.

The Platypus gets its name from its large webbed feet. Platypus means "animal with flat feet." Only the front feet are used for paddling when the platypus swims.

At first glance, the bill of a platypus looks like a duck's bill. But it is really very different. A duck's bill is hard and horny, but the platypus bill is soft and rubbery and packed with sensitive nerves.

A female platypus doesn't sit on her eggs like a bird. Instead, she wraps her body around them to keep them warm. It takes about 8 days for the eggs to hatch.

To insure privacy, the female blocks the tunnel with dirt.

The Spiny Ant-eater is also known as the Echidna (e-KID-nah). These curious little animals look very different from a platypus. They grow to be about 2 feet long (60 centimeters) and are covered on the back with sharp spines. They may live for a very long time—50 years and more.

When it feels threatened, the Spiny Ant-eater will sometimes roll up in a ball, with spines sticking out in all directions. At other times, it performs an amazing disappearing act, as shown at right.

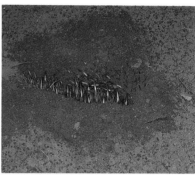

Spiny Ant-eaters have long and sticky tongues for catching their favorite foods—ants, termites, and other insects.

The speed with which a Spiny Ant-eater can bury itself in the ground is really astonishing. It digs in with all four of its feet, throwing dirt in all directions—and within 9 or 10 minutes it can be totally covered.

Like a beaver's tail, the tail of a platypus is long and flat. But it has long hair on top instead of scales. Fat is stored in the tail, and it is used as a rudder when the platypus swims.

Platypuses are famous for their incredible appetites. They only weigh about 4 pounds (2 kilograms), but they may eat 2 pounds of food (1 kilogram) every day. A single platypus can eat *12,500 worms* in a month. To get all of this food, a platypus must do a lot of diving. When it dives, it closes its eyes and ears, and uses its sensitive bill to feel around in the mud for food. Platypuses feed mostly at dawn and dusk. At times, they may stay under water without breathing for 10 minutes.

All mammals living today are descended from ancient egg-laying reptiles called therapsids (thur-AP-sidz), like the one shown here. Of all living mammals, the Platypus and Echidna are the most like these primitive reptiles.

Index